MW01229017

KNOWLEDGE
& ITS EFFECTS ON PURIFYING SOULS

SHAYKH 'ABDUR-RAZZAQ AL-ABBAD

مكتبة الإرشاد
Maktabatul-Irshad
PUBLICATIONS

ISBN: 978-1-6400-7889-5

First Edition: Jumada Thāni 1438 A.H. / March 2016 C.E.

Cover Design: Pario Studios, UK

Translation by Mustapha Abdul Hakim Lameu Misrī
Revision & Editing by ʿAbdullāh Omrān

Typesetting & formatting by Abū Sulaymān Muḥammad ʿAbdul-ʿAẓīm Ibn Joshua Baker

Subject: ʿAqīdah

Website: www.maktabatulirshad.com
E-mail: info@maktabatulirshad.com

مكتبة الإرشاد
Maktabatul-Irshad
PUBLICATIONS

Table of Contents

BRIEF BIOGRAPHY OF THE AUTHOR

His name: Shaykh 'Abdur-Razzaq al-Abbad.

He is the son of 'the *Muhaddith* of Madīnah Shaykh 'Abdul-Muhsin al 'Abbād al-Badr.

Birth: He was born on the 22nd day of *Dhul-Qa'dah*, 1382 AH in az-Zal'fi, Kingdom of Saudi Arabia. He currently resides in Madīnah.

Current Occupation: He is a member of the teaching staff at the Islāmic University of Madīnah.

Scholarly Certifications: Doctorate in '*Aqīdah*.

The Shaykh has authored books, papers of research, as well as numerous explanations in different disciplines. Among them are:

1. *Fiqh of Supplications & adh-Kār.*

2. *Hajj & Refinement of Souls.*

3. Explanation of 'Exemplary Principles' by Shaykh Ibn 'Uthaymīn (رَحِمَهُ ٱللَّه).

4. Explanation of the book: *The Principles of Names & Attributes*, authored by Shaykh-ul-Islām Ibn al-Qayyim (رَحِمَهُ ٱللَّه).

5. Explanation of the book: *Good Words*, authored by Shaykh-ul-Islām Ibn al-Qayyim (رَحِمَهُ ٱللَّه).

6. Explanation of the book, al-'Aqīdah *at-Tahāwiyyah*.

7. Explanation of the book: *Fuṣūl: Biography of the Messenger*, by Ibn Kathīr (رَحِمَهُ ٱللَّه).

8. An explanation of the book: *al-Adab-ul-Mufrad*, authored by Imām Bukhārī (رَحِمَهُ ٱللَّه).

He studied knowledge under a number of scholars. The most distinguished of them are:

1. His father the *'Allāmah* Shaykh 'Abdul-Muhsin al-Badr (حفظه ٱلله).

2. The *'Allāmah* Shaykh Ibn Bāz (رَحِمَهُ ٱللَّه).

3. The *'Allāmah* Shaykh Muḥammad Ibn Sālih al-'Uthaymīn (رَحِمَهُ ٱللَّه).

4. Shaykh 'Alī Ibn Nāsir al-Faqīhi (حفظه الله).

TRANSLITERATION TABLE

Consonants

ء	ʾ	د	d	ض	ḍ	ك	k
ب	b	ذ	dh	ط	ṭ	ل	l
ت	t	ر	r	ظ	ẓ	م	m
ث	th	ز	z	ع	ʿ	ن	n
ج	j	س	s	غ	gh	هـ	h
ح	ḥ	ش	sh	ف	f	و	w
خ	kh	ص	ṣ	ق	q	ي	y

Vowels

Short	◌َ	a	◌ِ	i	◌ُ	u
Long	◌َا	ā	◌ِي	ī	◌ُو	ū
Diphthongs	◌َوْ	aw	◌َيْ	ay

Arabic Symbols & their meanings

حفظه الله

May Allāh preserve him

رَضِىَاللَّهُعَنْهُ

May Allāh be pleased with him (i.e. a male companion of the Prophet Muḥammad)

سُبْحَانَهُوَتَعَالَى

Glorified & Exalted is Allāh

عَزَّوَجَلَّ

(Allāh) the Mighty & Sublime

تَبَارَكَوَتَعَالَى

(Allāh) the Blessed & Exalted

جَلَّوَعَلَا

(Allāh) the Sublime & Exalted

عَلَيْهِالصَّلَاةُوَالسَّلَامُ

May Allāh send Blessings & Safety upon him (i.e. a Prophet or Messenger)

صَلَّىاللَّهُعَلَيْهِوَعَلَىآلِهِوَسَلَّمَ

May Allāh send Blessings & Safety upon him and his

family (i.e. Du'ā sent when
mentioning the Prophet
Muḥammad)

رَحِمَهُ ٱللَّهُ

May Allāh have mercy on
him

رَضِيَاللَّهُ عَنْهُمْ

May Allāh be pleased with
them (i.e. Du'ā made for the
Companions of the Prophet
Muḥammad)

جَلَّ جَلَالُهُ

(Allāh) His Majesty is Exalted

رَضِيَاللَّهُ عَنْهَا

May Allāh be pleased with
her (i.e. a female companion
of the Prophet Muḥammad)

LECTURE

Indeed, all praise is due to Allāh. We praise Him, seek refuge with Him, and we seek His forgiveness. We seek refuge with Allāh from the evils of our souls and the mistakes in our actions. Whosoever Allāh guides, there is none who can misguide him, and whomsoever Allāh allows to be misguided, there is none who can guide him. And I testify that none has the right to be worshiped but Allāh alone, and I bear witness that Muḥammad (ﷺ) is His servant and Messenger, all prayers and blessings are upon him and his Companions.

As for what follows:

O, good brothers! Allāh made easy this meeting to take place in this blessed hour. I ask Allāh to bless it, make it for His sake, make it fruitful and include it on our scale of good deeds. What Allāh wills will come to pass! There is no power but with Allāh.

Before proceeding, I'd like to express my happiness and joy with this meeting because I'm in the presence of good brothers. I'd like to say that I was eager to meet you. I love the Algerian people for the sake of Allāh, and we are meeting here for His sake. That is the Grace of Allāh which He bestows on whom He is pleased with. And Allāh is the Owner of Great Bounty. The Algerian people are generous, brave and kind people. May Allāh reward all of us with guidance and help us to come closer to Allāh, the Almighty.

O, brothers! Our Prophet (صَلَّى اللهُ عَلَيْهِ وَسَلَّمَ) said,

لَا يَشْكُرُ اللهَ مَنْ لَا يَشْكُرُ النَّاسَ

"To be ungrateful to people is to be ungrateful to Allāh."[1]

The Prophet (صَلَّى اللهُ عَلَيْهِ وَسَلَّمَ) taught us to thank the one who does us a favor. Thus, I am grateful to all who participated in this meeting, especially those in the city of Qusantina, the city of knowledge and scholars. Also, I am grateful to the brothers who manage the Sabeel Ar-Rashad charitable association for their hospitability and endeavor. I ask Allāh to reward us all.

---

[1] Reported by Abu Dawud No. (4811). It is graded Sahih.

I am grateful to the brothers who came from long distances to attend this meeting and exerted effort to participate in it. I ask Allāh to reward us all and accept our good deeds.

With the help of Allāh, we can start our session asking Allāh's assistance and beseeching Him to grant us success. Our meeting today is about knowledge and its effect on purifying souls.

O, brothers! Knowledge is a light for its seeker. Allāh, the Almighty,

وَكَذَلِكَ أَوْحَيْنَآ إِلَيْكَ رُوحًا مِّنْ أَمْرِنَا ۚ مَا كُنتَ تَدْرِى مَا ٱلْكِتَـٰبُ وَلَا ٱلْإِيمَـٰنُ وَلَـٰكِن جَعَلْنَـٰهُ نُورًا نَّهْدِى بِهِۦ مَن نَّشَآءُ مِنْ عِبَادِنَا ۚ وَإِنَّكَ لَتَهْدِىٓ إِلَىٰ صِرَٰطٍ مُّسْتَقِيمٍ ۝

"And thus, we have sent to you (O Muḥammad ﷺ) Rūh (a Revelation and a Mercy) of Our Command. You Knew not what is the Book, nor what is Faith? But We have made it (this Qur'ān) a light wherewith We guide whosoever of Our slaves We will. And verily, you (O Muḥammad ﷺ) are indeed guiding (mankind) to the Straight Path (i.e. Allāh's Religion of Islāmic Monotheism)." [Sūrah Ash-Shura 42:52]

Knowledge is a light which illuminates the way for the knowledge seekers. It guides its seeker and removes any possible confusion. Allāh (سُبْحَانَهُوَتَعَالَى) says,

$$﴿ أَفَمَن يَمْشِى مُكِبًّا عَلَىٰ وَجْهِهِۦٓ أَهْدَىٰٓ أَمَّن يَمْشِى سَوِيًّا عَلَىٰ صِرَٰطٍ مُّسْتَقِيمٍ ۝ ﴾$$

"Is he who walks without seeing on his face, more rightly guided, or he who (sees and) walks on a Straight Way (i.e. Islāmic Monotheism)" [*Sūrah Al-Mulk* 67:22]

And Allāh says,

$$﴿ ۞ أَفَمَن يَعْلَمُ أَنَّمَآ أُنزِلَ إِلَيْكَ مِن رَّبِّكَ ٱلْحَقُّ كَمَنْ هُوَ أَعْمَىٰٓ ﴾$$

"Shall he then who knows that what has been revealed to you (O Muḥammad (صَلَّىٱللَّهُعَلَيْهِوَسَلَّمَ)) from your Lord is the truth be like him who is blind?" [*Sūrah Ar-Ra'd* 13:19]

And Allāh says,

$$﴿ قُلْ هَلْ يَسْتَوِى ٱلَّذِينَ يَعْلَمُونَ وَٱلَّذِينَ لَا يَعْلَمُونَ ﴾$$

"Say: "Are those who know equal to those who know not?" [*Sūrah Az-Zumar* 39:9]

There are a number of verses which share this same meaning.

Thus, seeking knowledge is a sign of goodness. The Prophet (ﷺ) said,

مَنْ يُرِدِ اللَّهُ بِهِ خَيْرًا يُفَقِّهْهُ فِي الدِّينِ

"When Allāh wishes good for someone, He bestows upon him the understanding of the religion."[2]

On the authority of Abū ad-Dardā' (رضي الله عنه) in Al-Musnad that the Prophet (ﷺ) said,

مَنْ سَلَكَ طَرِيقًا يَلْتَمِسُ فِيهِ عِلْمًا سَهَّلَ اللَّهُ لَهُ طَرِيقًا إِلَى الْجَنَّةِ، وَإِنَّ الْمَلَائِكَةَ لَتَضَعُ أَجْنِحَتَهَا رِضًا لِطَالِبِ الْعِلْمِ، وَإِنَّ طَالِبَ الْعِلْمِ يَسْتَغْفِرُ لَهُ مَنْ فِي السَّمَاءِ وَالْأَرْضِ حَتَّى الْحِيتَانِ فِي الْمَاءِ، وَإِنَّ فَضْلَ الْعَالِمِ عَلَى الْعَابِدِ كَفَضْلِ الْقَمَرِ عَلَى سَائِرِ الْكَوَاكِبِ، إِنَّ الْعُلَمَاءَ هُمْ وَرَثَةُ الْأَنْبِيَاءِ ؛ إِنَّ الْأَنْبِيَاءَ لَمْ يُوَرِّثُوا دِينَارًا وَلَا دِرْهَمًا إِنَّمَا وَرَّثُوا الْعِلْمَ فَمَنْ أَخَذَهُ أَخَذَ بِحَظٍّ وَافِرٍ

"He who follows a path in a quest for knowledge, Allāh will make the path of Jannah easy for him. The angels lower their

---

[2] Reported by Ibn Majah (1/225). It is graded Sahih.

wings over the seeker of knowledge, being pleased with what he does. The inhabitants of the heavens and the earth and the even the fish in the depths of the oceans seek the forgiveness for him. The superiority of the learned man over the devout worshipper is like that of the full moon to the rest of the stars (i.e., in brightness). The learned are the heirs of the Prophets who bequeath neither dinar nor dirham but only that of knowledge; and he who acquires it, has in fact acquired an abundant portion."[3]

So, there are many aḥādīth known by the knowledge seekers and the lay people about the value of knowledge, its honorable status and the high rank of its seekers.

The more the servant strives to seek knowledge for the sake of Allāh, the more purified his soul will be. Only knowledge makes souls purified. Allāh, the Almighty, says,

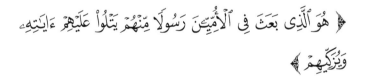

---

[3] Reported by Ibn Majah (1/228); and Reported by at-Tirmidhi No. (2646). It is graded Sahih.

"He it is Who sent among the unlettered ones a Messenger (Muḥammad (ﷺ)) from among themselves, reciting to them His Verses, purifying them (from the filth of disbelief and polytheism)." [*Sūrah Al-Jumuʿah* 62:2]

In this ayah, purification will be reached through the recitation of some Āyāt and studying Allāh's Revelation. Allāh, the Almighty, says,

$$﴿ إِنَّ هَٰذَا ٱلْقُرْءَانَ يَهْدِى لِلَّتِى هِىَ أَقْوَمُ ﴾$$

"Verily, this Qur'ān guides to that which is most just and right." [*Sūrah Al-Isrā'* 17:9]

Allāh also says,

$$﴿ وَنُنَزِّلُ مِنَ ٱلْقُرْءَانِ مَا هُوَ شِفَآءٌ وَرَحْمَةٌ لِّلْمُؤْمِنِينَ ﴾$$

"And We send down from the Qur'ān that which is a healing and mercy to those who believe (in Islāmic Monotheism and act on it)." [*Sūrah Al-Isrā'* 17:82]

Allāh says,

"Say: 'It is for those who believe, a guide and healing.'" [*Sūrah Fussilat* 41:44]

Also, Allāh, the Almighty, says,

$$\text{﴿ إِنَّ فِي ذَٰلِكَ لَذِكْرَىٰ لِمَن كَانَ لَهُۥ قَلْبٌ أَوْ أَلْقَى ٱلسَّمْعَ وَهُوَ شَهِيدٌ ۝ ﴾}$$

"Verily, therein is indeed a reminder for him who has a heart or gives ear while he is heedful." [*Sūrah Qāf* 50:37]

Allāh says,

$$\text{﴿ قُلْ إِنَّمَآ أُنذِرُكُم بِٱلْوَحْيِ ﴾}$$

"Say (O Muḥammad (ﷺ)): "I warn you only by the revelation (from Allāh and not by the opinion of the religious scholars and others)." [*Sūrah Al-Anbiyā'* 21:45]

Allāh also says,

$$\text{﴿ فَذَكِّرْ بِٱلْقُرْءَانِ مَن يَخَافُ وَعِيدِ ۝ ﴾}$$

"But warn by the Qur'ān him who fears My Threat." [*Sūrah Qāf* 50:45]

And many verses are indicating the same meaning.

When one handles this significantly elaborate topic of soul purification and its aspects in light of verses and authentic aḥādīth, one deduces solid principles and comprehensive foundational rules that pave the way to purifying souls.

The most significant principle in this respect is that soul purification is a divine blessing. Allāh only sanctifies whom He wills. Allāh, the Almighty, says,

﴿ أَلَمْ تَرَ إِلَى ٱلَّذِينَ يُزَكُّونَ أَنفُسَهُم بَلِ ٱللَّهُ يُزَكِّي مَن يَشَآءُ ﴾

"Have you not seen those who claim sanctity for themselves? Nay, but Allāh sanctifies whom He pleases." [*Sūrah An-Nisā' 4:49*]

Allāh says,

﴿ وَلَوْلَا فَضْلُ ٱللَّهِ عَلَيْكُمْ وَرَحْمَتُهُ مَا زَكَىٰ مِنكُم مِّنْ أَحَدٍ أَبَدًا وَلَٰكِنَّ ٱللَّهَ يُزَكِّي مَن يَشَآءُ ﴾

"And had it not been for the Grace of Allāh and His Mercy on you, not one of you would ever have been pure from sins. But Allāh purifies (guides to Islām) whom He wills, and

Allāh is All-Hearer, All-Knower." [*Sūrah An-Nūr* 24:21]

Allāh also says,

﴿ يَمُنُّونَ عَلَيْكَ أَنْ أَسْلَمُوا۟ قُل لَّا تَمُنُّوا۟ عَلَىَّ إِسْلَـٰمَكُم بَلِ ٱللَّهُ يَمُنُّ عَلَيْكُمْ أَنْ هَدَىٰكُمْ لِلْإِيمَـٰنِ إِن كُنتُمْ صَـٰدِقِينَ ۝ ﴾

"They regard as a favor upon you (O Muḥammad (ﷺ)) that they have embraced Islām. Say: 'Count not your Islām as a favor to me. Nay, but Allāh has conferred a favor upon you, that He has guided you to the Faith if you indeed are true.'" [*Sūrah Al-Hujurāt* 49:17]

Allāh, the Almighty, says,

﴿ وَلَـٰكِنَّ ٱللَّهَ حَبَّبَ إِلَيْكُمُ ٱلْإِيمَـٰنَ وَزَيَّنَهُۥ فِى قُلُوبِكُمْ وَكَرَّهَ إِلَيْكُمُ ٱلْكُفْرَ وَٱلْفُسُوقَ وَٱلْعِصْيَانَ أُو۟لَـٰٓئِكَ هُمُ ٱلرَّٰشِدُونَ ۝ فَضْلًا مِّنَ ٱللَّهِ وَنِعْمَةً وَٱللَّهُ عَلِيمٌ حَكِيمٌ ۝ ﴾

"But Allāh has endeared the Faith to you and has beautified it in your hearts, and has made disbelief, wickedness, and disobedience (to Allāh and His Messenger (ﷺ)) hateful to you. These! They are the rightly guided ones.

(This is) a Grace from Allāh and His Favor. And Allāh is All-Knowing, All-Wise." [*Sūrah Al-Hujurāt* 49:7-8]

There are many verses in this regard. Also, the Prophet's Companions (رَضِيَٱللَّهُعَنْهُمْ) said,

وَلَا صُمْنَا وَلَا صَلَّيْنَا   وَاللَّهِ لَوْلَا اللَّهُ مَا اهْتَدَيْنَا

"By Allāh, without Him, we wouldn't be guided nor were we to fast nor pray."

So, favor and grace are only from Allāh Who can guide to the Straight Path,

﴿ أَفَمَن زُيِّنَ لَهُۥ سُوٓءُ عَمَلِهِۦ فَرَءَاهُ حَسَنًا فَإِنَّ ٱللَّهَ يُضِلُّ مَن يَشَآءُ وَيَهْدِى مَن يَشَآءُ فَلَا تَذْهَبْ نَفْسُكَ عَلَيْهِمْ حَسَرَٰتٍ ﴾

"Is he, then, to whom the evil of his deeds made fair-seeming, so that he considers it as good (equal to one who is rightly guided)? Verily, Allāh sends astray whom He wills, and guides whom He wills. So, destroy not yourself (O Muḥammad (صَلَّىٱللَّهُعَلَيْهِوَسَلَّمَ)) in sorrow for them." [*Sūrah Fatir* 35:8]

The Prophet (صَلَّىٱللَّهُعَلَيْهِوَسَلَّمَ) has instilled this principle in the souls of the companion. He used to say in Friday speeches,

إِنَّ الْحَمْدَ لِلَّهِ نَحْمَدُهُ وَنَسْتَعِينُهُ مَنْ يَهْدِهِ اللَّهُ فَلَا مُضِلَّ لَهُ وَمَنْ
يُضْلِلْ فَلَا هَادِيَ لَهُ وَأَشْهَدُ أَنْ لَا إِلَهَ إِلَّا اللَّهُ وَحْدَهُ لَا شَرِيكَ لَهُ
وَأَنَّ مُحَمَّدًا عَبْدُهُ وَرَسُولُهُ

**"Praise be to Allāh; we seek His help.
Whomsoever Allāh guides will never be led
astray, and whomsoever Allāh allows to go
astray, no one can guide. I bear witness that
there is none worthy of worship but Allāh
(Alone with no partners) and I bear witness
that Muhammad is His servant and
Messenger."[4]**

This is known as the speech of need which combines
the principles of the religion and the rules of *Sharī'ah*.
Understanding this Khutbah will have a great
influence; it was a reason for guiding a tribe to Islām.
We can find this in a story related by Imām Muslim
(رَحِمَهُ اللَّهُ) that narrates the embrace of Islām by Dimad
Al-Azdi (رَضِيَ اللَّهُ عَنْهُ):

وذلك أنّ ضماداً كان في جاهليته راقياً يشتغل برقية الناس
ومن كان منهم مصاباً بمسٍّ أو جنون أو نحو ذلك ، وكان
مُشتهرا بالرّقية ، يقول : قدِمتُ مكة فكنتُ كلما مررت
بطريق في مكة سمعت "إنّ محمداً مجنون" ، فقلت : إنِّي رجل

---

4 Reported by Sunan an-Nasā'ī No. (3278). It is graded Sahih.

21 | P a g e

راقٍ ، وإنَّ الله شَفى على يديَّ من شاء من عباده ، لـئِن لقيت هذا الرجل لأُرْقِينَه لعل الله يشفيه على يدي ، يقول ثم إنَّـني لقيت محمداً – أي النبي عليه الصلاة والسلام – فقلت له : إنَّـني رجل راقٍ وإنَّ الله شفى على يدي من شاء فهل لك في ذلك ؟ – تحب أنْ أرقيك ؟ ، يخاطب بذلك النبي عليه الصلاة والسلام بسبب الدعاية الآثمة الكبيرة الواسعة التي تُحاك حوله – فقال النبي عليه الصلاة والسلام : ((إنّ الحمد لله نحمده ونستعينه ، ونعوذ بالله من شرور أنفسنا وسيئات أعمالنا من يهده الله فلا مضل له ، ومن يضلل فلا هادي له ، وأشهد أنّ لا إله إلا الله وحده لا شريك له ، وأشهد أنّ محمداً عبده ورسوله)) ، قال فقلت له : أعِـد عليّ كلامك هذا – أعجبه الكلام وأثَّـر فِيه – فأعاده النبي عليه الصلاة والسلام . قال ضمام فقلت له : لقد سمعتُ كلام السّحرة والكهنة وما هذا من كلامهم ، وسمعتُ كلام المجانين وما هذا من كلامهم ، سمعتُ كلام الشعراء ما هذا من كلامهم ، ووالله إنّ كلامك هذا قد بلغ قاموس البحر – أعظم بحر ، يعني كلمتك دخلت في الصميم – أعطني يدك أبايعك على الإسلام ، فقال له النبي عليه الصلاة

والسلام : ((وعلى قومك ؟)) قال : وعلى قومي . لأنّه كان رئيس وسيد قومه .

"Dimad was healing people who were inflicted with craziness and charm. He said about himself: when I came to Makkah, I heard people speaking about Muḥammad (ﷺ), calling him a mad person. I said, 'I can heal him, Allāh helped me protect many people from charm, so if I met Muḥammad, I would heal him.' He continued, 'I met Muḥammad, the Prophet (ﷺ) and told him that I can heal and that Allāh helped me heal many people; can I help you be protected?' He was speaking in this manner with the Prophet (ﷺ) based on the heresies that had been spread about him.

The Prophet (ﷺ) said to him: 'Praise be to Allāh, we praise Him, and we seek His help. We seek refuge with Allāh from the evil of our own souls and our bad deeds. Whomsoever Allāh guides will never be led astray and whomsoever Allāh allows to go astray, no one can guide. I bear witness that there is none worthy of worship but Allāh (Alone with no partners), and I bear witness that Muḥammad is His servant and Messenger.' Dimad said, 'Could you repeat these words.' He admired those words, so the Prophet (ﷺ) repeated them. Dimad said, 'I have heard the words of magicians and priests and the words of madmen and poets, but these are not their words; your words influenced me a lot. Let me give a pledge to embrace Islām.' The Prophet (ﷺ) said, 'And your tribe?' He said, 'And my tribe" because he was the chief of his tribe."

This speech was the reason he embraced Islām. It is based on high principles and rooted in foundational guidelines which one should pay lots of attention to benefit from them. These principles refer to many aspects that should be considered, such as:

$$ وَ نَعُوذُ بِاللهِ مِنْ شُرُورِ أَنْفُسِنَا $$

"We seek refuge with Allāh from the evil of our own souls."

And,

$$ مَنْ يَهْدِهِ اللهُ فَلَا مُضِلَّ لَهُ $$

"Whomsoever Allāh guides will never be led astray."

And so on.

So, guidance and soul purification are a grace from Allāh. He guides and sanctifies whom He wills, with no partner. Thus, soul purification is the most significant principle in this regard. It cannot be sought from anyone but Allāh because no one can grant it but Him. The servant should endeavor to better his connection with Allāh. He should be sincere and ask Allāh to guide him and set him right. Allāh, the Almighty, does not reject the servant's invocations and supplications. He says,

$$\text{﴿ وَإِذَا سَأَلَكَ عِبَادِى عَنِّى فَإِنِّى قَرِيبٌ ۖ أُجِيبُ دَعْوَةَ ٱلدَّاعِ إِذَا دَعَانِ ۖ فَلْيَسْتَجِيبُوا۟ لِى وَلْيُؤْمِنُوا۟ بِى لَعَلَّهُمْ يَرْشُدُونَ ۝ ﴾}$$

"And when My slaves ask you (O Muḥammad (ﷺ)) concerning Me, then (answer them), I am indeed near (to them by My Knowledge). I respond to the invocations of the supplicant when he calls on Me (without any mediator or intercessor). So, let them obey Me and believe in Me, so that they may be led aright." [*Sūrah Al-Baqarah* 2:186]

Brothers, this draws attention to the importance of the invocation in this respect. Some of the Salaf (رَحِمَهُمُ ٱللَّهُ) said,

"I thought about the means of goodness and found out they are plenty, and I realized that all of them depend on Allāh. At this point, I became sure that invocation is the means for every goodness."

The faithful servant shall invocate and supplicate to Allāh to guide him, set his heart right, sanctify him, guide him to the Straight Path, save him from the path of misguidance, not to neglect him and so on. The Prophet (ﷺ) used to say the following invocation frequently,

رَبَّنَا آتِنَا فِي الدُّنْيَا حَسَنَةً وَفِي الْآخِرَةِ حَسَنَةً وَقِنَا عَذَابَ

"Our Lord! Give us (Your Bounties) in this world and the Hereafter and save us from the punishment of the Hellfire."[5]

Another invocation he used to say abundantly,

يَا مُقَلِّبَ الْقُلُوبِ ثَبِّتْ قَلْبِي عَلَى دِينِكَ

"O Changer of the hearts! Make my heart firm upon Your religion."[6]

---

[5] Reported by Muslim No. (2690). It is graded Sahih.
[6] Reported by at-Tirmidhi No. (3522). It is graded Hasan.

يَا رَسُولَ اللهِ مَا أَكْثَرَ مَا دُعَاءَكَ يَا مُقَلِّبَ الْقُلُوبِ ثَبِّتْ قَلْبِي عَلَى دِينِكَ قَالَ يَا أُمَّ سَلَمَةَ إِنَّهُ لَيْسَ آدَمِيٌّ إِلَّا وَقَلْبُهُ بَيْنَ أُصْبُعَيْنِ مِنْ أَصَابِعِ اللهِ فَمَنْ شَاءَ أَقَامَ وَمَنْ شَاءَ أَزَاغَ

"Umm Salamah (رَضِىَ ٱللَّهُ عَنْهَا) said to the Prophet (صَلَّى ٱللَّهُ عَلَيْهِ وَسَلَّمَ), "O Messenger of Allāh! You are saying this supplication most frequently, 'O Changer of the hearts! Make my heart firm upon Your religion.' He said to Umm Salamah,

"Verily, there is no human being except that his heart is between Two Fingers of the Fingers of Allāh, so whomsoever He wills to be guided will be steadfast and whomever He wills to be otherwise, He causes to deviate."

And in the Qur'ān,

﴿ رَبَّنَا لَا تُزِغْ قُلُوبَنَا بَعْدَ إِذْ هَدَيْتَنَا وَهَبْ لَنَا مِن لَّدُنكَ رَحْمَةً إِنَّكَ أَنتَ ٱلْوَهَّابُ ۝ ﴾

"(They say): "Our Lord! Let not our hearts deviate (from the truth) after You have guided us, and grant us mercy from You. Truly, you are the Bestower." [*Sūrah 'Āli-'Imrān* 3:8]

It is also found in the supplication of Ibrāhīm (عَلَيْهِ ٱلصَّلَاةُ وَٱلسَّلَامُ),

﴿ رَبِّ ٱجْعَلْنِي مُقِيمَ ٱلصَّلَوٰةِ وَمِن ذُرِّيَّتِي ﴾

"O, my Lord! Make me one who performs As-Salāt (Iqamat-as-Salāt), and (also) from my offspring, our Lord!" [*Sūrah Ibrāhīm* 14:40]

"Make me one who performs,"

You cannot perform prayer unless Allāh helps you perform it and the same goes for one's offspring. Allāh says,

﴿ رَبِّ ٱجْعَلْنِي مُقِيمَ ٱلصَّلَوٰةِ وَمِن ذُرِّيَّتِي ﴾

"O, my Lord! Make me one who performs As-Salāt (Iqamat-as-Salāt), and (also) from my offspring, our Lord!" [*Sūrah Ibrāhīm* 14:40]

It is related in Sahīh Muslim,

اللَّهُمَّ أَصْلِحْ لِي دِينِي الَّذِي هُوَ عِصْمَةُ أَمْرِي ، وَأَصْلِحْ لِي دُنْيَايَ الَّتِي فِيهَا مَعَاشِي ، وَأَصْلِحْ لِي آخِرَتِي الَّتِي فِيهَا مَعَادِي ، وَاجْعَلْ الْحَيَاةَ زِيَادَةً لِي فِي كُلِّ خَيْرٍ ، وَاجْعَلْ الْمَوْتَ رَاحَةً لِي مِنْ كُلِّ شَرٍّ

"O Allāh, make my religion easy for me by virtue of which my affairs are protected, set right for me my world where my life exists, make good for me my Hereafter which is my

resort to which I have to return, and make my life prone to perform all types of good, and make death a comfort for me from every evil."[7]

Furthermore, the invocation to be said by the distressed,

اللَّهُمَّ رَحْمَتَكَ أَرْجُو فَلَا تَكِلْنِي إِلَى نَفْسِي طَرْفَةَ عَيْنٍ وَأَصْلِحْ لِي شَأْنِي كُلَّهُ لَا إِلَهَ إِلَّا أَنْتَ

"O Allāh! Your mercy is what I hope for. Do not abandon me to myself for an instant, but put all my affairs in good order for me. There is no god worthy of worship but You."[8]

Concerning soul purification, in particular, there was a hadīth related by Zayd ibn Arkam (رَضِيَاللَّهُعَنْهُ) in Sahīh Muslim, the Prophet (صَلَّىاللَّهُعَلَيْهِوَسَلَّمَ) said,

اللَّهُمَّ آتِ نَفْسِي تَقْوَاهَا ، وَزَكِّهَا أَنْتَ خَيْرُ مَنْ زَكَّاهَا ؛ أَنْتَ وَلِيُّهَا وَمَوْلَاهَا

"O Allāh! Grant me the sense of piety and purify my soul as You are the Best to purify it.

---

[7] Reported by Muslim No. (2720). It is graded Sahih.
[8] Reported by Abu Dawud No. (5090). Shaykh al-Albaani graded it Hasan in its chain of narrators.

You are its Guardian and its Protecting
Friend." [9]

The Prophet (ﷺ) supplicated to Allāh with
these two Great Names: Guardian and Protecting
Friend; both of these names refer to the special
guardianship of Allāh over the believers and how He
helps His servant. He supplicates to Allāh with these
two great Names to grant him the sense of piety and
purify his soul. The soul cannot be purified but with
the help of Allāh. We ask Allāh, the Most Bountiful,
the Lord of the Great Throne, to grant us the sense of
piety and to purify our souls. He is the best to purify
it. He is its Guardian and Protecting Friend.

Addressing self-purification in light of the verses and
aḥādīth has many aspects. In this meeting, we will
tackle many important aspects and great rules taken
from the Book of Allāh and the Sunnah of the Prophet
(ﷺ); all of which revolve around self-
purification.

First of all, we will speak about the human self, its
essence, and characteristics. We will mention some
examples given by the scholars concerning the human
self and how self-purification needs intensive and
continuous care of this self to bar it from destruction.

---

[9] Reported by Sunan an-Nasā'ī No. (5458). It is graded Sahih.

There are three prominent types of soul mentioned in the Qur'ān: the content soul, the evil soul, and the self-reproaching soul. These qualities refer to different modes one's soul goes through.

If the soul is filled with belief, remembrance of Allāh and His worship, it is called *"the peaceful soul."*

﴿ ٱلَّذِينَ ءَامَنُواْ وَتَطْمَئِنُّ قُلُوبُهُم بِذِكْرِ ٱللَّهِ أَلَا بِذِكْرِ ٱللَّهِ تَطْمَئِنُّ ٱلْقُلُوبُ ۞ ٱلَّذِينَ ءَامَنُواْ وَعَمِلُواْ ٱلصَّٰلِحَٰتِ طُوبَىٰ لَهُمْ وَحُسْنُ مَئَابٍ ۞ ﴾

"Those who believe (in the Oneness of Allāh – Islāmic Monotheism), and whose hearts find rest in the remembrance of Allāh. Verily, in the remembrance of Allāh do hearts find rest. Those who believe (in the Oneness of Allah - Islamic Monotheism), and work righteousness, Tuba (it means all kinds of happiness or name of a tree in Paradise) is for them and a beautiful place of (final) return." [*Sūrah Ar-Ra'd* 13:28-29]

But if the soul urges one to commit bad deeds, sins, and lead him to places of fornication, it is called *"the evil soul."*

If the soul reproaches, it is called *"the self-reproaching soul."* It blames one for committing sins or negligence of obedience. It is further subdivided into two divisions according to what is mentioned by the scholars:

- It may be an evil soul who blames one for not doing bad deeds.
- One which blames one for not doing good deeds. This is related to the peaceful soul.

These three types of the soul are interchangeable in the sense that they may occur alternatively in a single day. Everyone can realize such fluctuation which is caused by thoughts. When one remembers Allāh or attends a learning session, he is elevated towards virtuousness because of these thoughts, and his self finds peace. A lot of people talk about themselves saying, "When I enter the Masjid for praying, seeking knowledge and remembering Allāh, I find peace in myself." This tranquility is caused by these good deeds. However, if one goes to the places where vices, sins, and corruption are committed, he finds his soul has become evil.

O, brothers! This indicates that the soul needs soul searching and self-combat, which is a kind of striving in Allāh's Cause. The Prophet (ﷺ) said in the Farewell Pilgrimage,

أَلَا أُخْبِرُكُمْ بِالْمُؤْمِنِ ؟ مَنْ أَمِنَهُ النَّاسُ عَلَى أَمْوَالِهِمْ وَأَنْفُسِهِمْ ،

وَالْمُسْلِمُ مَنْ سَلِمَ النَّاسُ مِنْ لِسَانِهِ وَيَدِهِ، وَالْمُجَاهِدُ مَنْ جَاهَدَ

نَفْسَهُ فِي طَاعَةِ اللَّهِ ، وَالْمُهَاجِرُ مَنْ هَجَرَ الْخَطَايَا وَالذُّنُوبَ

"Do you know [what makes] a believer? The believer is the one from whom the people's wealth and lives are safe. The Muslim is the one from whose tongue and hand the (other) Muslims are safe. The Mujāhid is one who strives against his own soul, and the Muhajir is the one who forsakes mistakes and sins."

There is no doubt that this is striving against the desires of the human soul. Certainly, this is difficult, but if one tries hard, he will become self-purified with the help of Allāh.

O, brothers! There are two examples given by two great scholars about self-purification:

1. Imām Ājurry (رَحِمَهُٱللَّه) in his book "Adab An-Nufūs" which is small in size but great in value.

2. Imām Ibn Al-Qayyim (رَحِمَهُٱللَّه) in his book "Madārij As-Sālikīn."

Let's discuss first Imām Ājurry's example! I urge attentive consideration to the example's connotations and dimensions. Indeed, examples make meanings more clear and concrete.

Ājurrī (رَحِمَهُ اللَّهُ) said,

> "Let me give you a clear example you're all aware of. The soul is like the beautiful colt between the horses. If one looks at it, he will be taken by its beauty. But the learned people tell its owner that this colt cannot be used without proper training. So, it will be useful for all sorts of things after which its trainer will appreciate all the training it took to reach this level. Otherwise, it would be neglected when the need arises due to lack of training. If this colt's owner accepted this advice, believing it is a good opinion, he would give it to a tamer to train it.
>
> This tamer should be learned and patient so that the colt owner will make use of it. But if the tamer does not know how to train horses, he will spoil this horse, become exhausted in vain, and none can benefit from it. In contrast, if the tamer knows about the taming of horses, yet lacks the necessary patience to train, and replaced the training with spending time in self-entertainment, he will spoil this colt after which it would be ineligible for use. If the owner is the tamer, he will regret at a time when regret would be of no avail. And when

he realizes that others achieved their goals, while he failed due to impatience after having knowledge, he will blame and reproach it saying, 'Why did you dawdle?' Such impatience causes me distress. It is Allāh (Alone) Whose help can be sought. Know and think about this example, and you will succeed."

And then Imām Ājurrī (رَحِمَهُ أللَّه) cited from Wahb ibn Monabih, one of the successors of the Prophet's companions, who said, "The soul is like the livestock, faith is its manager, good deeds are its driver. The soul is stubborn. If its leader dawdled, it would rebel against its driver, and if its driver idled, it would get lost."

In this example, Imām Ājurrī (رَحِمَهُ أللَّه) clarified that the soul needs its trainer to be patient and learned, one who knows how to set it right and sanctify it in light of the Book of Allāh and the Sunnah of the Prophet (صَلَّى أللَّهُ عَلَيْهِ وَسَلَّم); and whoever dawdles, he will be sorry.

The second example is mentioned by Imām Ibn Al-Qayyim (رَحِمَهُ أللَّه) in his book "Madārij As-Sālikīn," is as follows,

"The soul it stands as a barren mountain in one's path to Allāh. Everyone has to cross this mountain to reach the end. Some people find difficulty in crossing, and some find it easy to reach. It is easy for the one whom Allāh makes it easy for. In this mountain, one can find valleys, trails, barriers, lowlands, thorns, boxthorns, brambles and thieves which hinder the worshippers, especially the ones who stand to pray at night. If they do not have the basics of belief and lamps of truthfulness enlightened by the oil of worship, these barriers and drawbacks will hinder their way to Allāh. Most of the worshippers in this path have stopped when they couldn't continue to cross the obstacles.

Upon this mountain, you can find Satan warns people to climb this mountain and frightens them. So, the difficulty in climbing, the Satan upon its mountaintop, the weakness of the worshipper and his intention; all of this results in failure, may Allāh protect us. Whenever the worshipper climbs this mountain, Satan sits atop the mountain to warn and frighten him. When the worshipper reaches the mountaintop, these fears will turn to certainty. At that time, worship will be easy, and the barriers will be removed, so the worshipper will see a wide road which leads to lodgings upon which there are landmarks and dwellings prepared for Allāh's worshippers. To reach success, the servant should have determination, patience, bravery and firmness.

Grace is (entirely) in Allāh's Hand to bestow on whomsoever He wills. And Allāh is the Owner of Great Bounty."

O, brothers! Both of the examples above clarify the state of the human soul and that the soul needs to be cultivated, educated and civilized. Otherwise, it will be led astray. It is better that one keeps his deeds in check while being in this worldly life before Allāh asks him in the Hereafter. Umar Ibn Al-Khattāb (رَضِيَ اللَّهُ عَنْهُ) said,

"Bring yourself to account before you are taken to account. Weigh your deeds before the Day of Judgment, prepare yourself for the Greater Judgment. You shall be brought to Judgment on this Day, and no secret of you will be hidden."

It is better that the servant should bring himself to account before he is taken to account on the Day of Judgment. To bring oneself to account in this worldly life is better because it leads to doing good deeds and setting right one's affairs. This causes the soul to succeed.

There are many quotations of the Salaf (رَحِمَهُمُ اللَّهُ) that urge us to bring the soul to account:

Al-Hassan Al-Basri (رَحِمَهُ اللَّهُ) said,

"The servant will be good as long as he blames himself and brings himself into account."

Maymūn Ibn Mehran (رَحِمَهُٱللَّه) said,

"The servant will be pious when he brings himself to account as partners do, and it is said that the soul is like the traitor partner who wastes your money if you do not bring him to account."

Al-Hassan (رَحِمَهُٱللَّه) said,

"The believer should bring himself to account. Accounting on the Day of Judgment will be less intense for people who brought themselves into account in this worldly life. In contrast, it will be more severe for people who do not bring themselves into account in this life. When a believer is impressed by something, he will say, 'By Allāh, I desire that and I need to have it, but I cannot have it just yet.' When he commits a mistake, he says to himself, 'I never wanted to do that. I will never do it again.' True believers are those whom the Qur'ān has influenced to abstain from what it instructs them to refrain from, which is their destruction. The believer is like a captive in this worldly life who tries to set himself free, but he cannot be assured until the Day of Resurrection. He will know that he will be asked about his hearing, sight, tongue and organs. He will be held accountable to all of them."

There are many texts by the Salaf (رَحِمَهُمُاللَّهُ) in this regard.

Purifying the soul is important in this time when temptations may turn one away from goodness and make him indulge in evil deeds. Abdullāh Ibn Al-Mubārak (رَحِمَهُاللَّهُ), one of the successors of the Prophet's Companions (رَضِىَاللَّهُعَنْهُ), said at his time,

"In the past, the righteous people were doing good deeds voluntarily. Our own selves, unfortunately, do good deeds with reluctance; and hence we should force them to do good deeds."

He said this at a time of righteousness, what about our era when some temptations and seductions prevent one from worship.

Next point: Let's talk about the essence of self-purification and how to achieve self-purification? One can sum this up in three points:

First: The basis of self-purification is belief in Allāh, monotheism, faithfulness and implementing the testimony that there is none who has the right to be worshiped but Allāh alone. Its implementation requires [the combination] of faithfulness and the Oneness of Allāh in all aspects of humility, submission, loyalty and obedience and all types of worship. This is the basis of self-purification.

The soul that does good deeds is like a blessed tree, which apparently must stand on roots. Allāh, the Almighty, says,

$$ ﴿ أَلَمْ تَرَ كَيْفَ ضَرَبَ ٱللَّهُ مَثَلًا كَلِمَةً طَيِّبَةً كَشَجَرَةٍ طَيِّبَةٍ أَصْلُهَا ثَابِتٌ وَفَرْعُهَا فِى ٱلسَّمَآءِ ۞ تُؤْتِىٓ أُكُلَهَا كُلَّ حِينٍ بِإِذْنِ رَبِّهَا ﴾ $$

"See you not how Allāh sets forth a parable? A goodly word as a goodly tree, whose root is firmly fixed, and its branches (reach) to the sky (i.e. very high). Giving its fruit at all times, by the Leave of its Lord." [*Sūrah Ibrāhīm* 14:24-25]

So, self-purification depends fundamentally on monotheism and sincerity. Allāh (سُبْحَانَهُوَتَعَالَى) says,

$$ ﴿ قَدْ أَفْلَحَ مَن زَكَّىٰهَا ۞ وَقَدْ خَابَ مَن دَسَّىٰهَا ۞ ﴾ $$

"Indeed, he succeeds who purifies his ownself (i.e. obeys and performs all that Allāh ordered, by following the true Faith of Islāmic

Monotheism and by doing righteous good deeds). And indeed, he fails who corrupts his ownself (i.e. disobeys what Allāh has ordered by rejecting the true Faith of Islāmic Monotheism or by following polytheism or by doing every kind of evil, wicked deeds)." [*Sūrah Ash-Shams* 91:9-10]

And Allāh (سُبْحَانَهُوَتَعَالَى) says,

"And woe to Al-Mushrikūn (the disbelievers in the Oneness of Allah, polytheists, idolaters, etc.) Those who give not the Zakāt." [*Sūrah Fussilat* 41:6-7]

Ibn 'Abbas (رَضِيَاللَّهُعَنْهُ) commented on the verse,

"It refers to those who do not testify that none has the right to be worshiped but Allāh."

Mujahid (رَضِيَاللَّهُعَنْهُ) said,

"It refers to those who do not sanctify their deeds."

In other words, their deeds are not righteous. In the earlier quotation, it is probable that he was referring to those who commit minor polytheism which is showing off.

Allāh (سُبْحَانَهُوَتَعَالَ) says in the story of Mūsā
(عَلَيْهِٱلصَّلَاةُوَٱلسَّلَامُ) with Fir'aun (Pharaoh),

﴿ فَقُلْ هَل لَّكَ إِلَىٰٓ أَن تَزَكَّىٰ ۱۸ ﴾

**"And say (to him): "Would you purify yourself
(from the sin of disbelief by becoming a
disbeliever)?"** [*Sūrah an-Nāzi'āt* 79:18]

Purify yourself by means of faith and monotheism.

Self-purification is like a blessed, fruitful tree based
on monotheism and sincerity. The firmer one's belief,
honesty, and monotheism, the more steadily this will
help the tree grow and make it fruitful with delicious
and good fruits.

<u>Second</u>: The soul can be purified by the requisites of
Islām and worshipping Allāh by way of sticking to
His orders and abstaining from His prohibitions.

Self-purification has two aspects expressed by its
linguistic root and religious connotations found in the
respective Sharī'ah texts. These two aspects are
purification and growth. In the same lines, giving
charity is also called *purification* because it purifies
one's money,

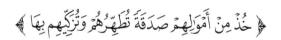

﴿ خُذْ مِنْ أَمْوَٰلِهِمْ صَدَقَةً تُطَهِّرُهُمْ وَتُزَكِّيهِم بِهَا ﴾

"Take Sadaqah (Zakāt, charity) from their wealth to purify them and sanctify them with it." [*Sūrah At-Tawbah* 9:103]

It is a reason for the growth of money. The purification aspect is achieved through the turning away from sins, while the growth aspect is achieved by way of doing good deeds and acts of worship.

Soul purification is considered purification and beautification. It is to purify the soul from vices and evil deeds and beautify the soul with acts of worship and righteous good deeds.

Performing prayer is a kind of Soul purification. Allāh (عَزَّوَجَلَّ) says,

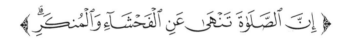

"Verily, As-Salah (the prayer) prevents from Al-Fahsha' (i.e. great sins of every kind, unlawful sexual intercourse) and Al-Munkar (i.e. disbelief, polytheism, and every kind of evil, wicked deed)." [*Sūrah Al-'Ankabūt* 29:45]

Related by Bukhari and Muslim, on the authority of Abū Hurayrah (رَضِيَاللَّهُعَنْهُ) that the Prophet (صَلَّىاللَّهُعَلَيْهِوَسَلَّمَ) said,

أَرَأَيْتُمْ لَوْ أَنَّ نَهْرًا بِبَابِ أَحَدِكُمْ يَغْتَسِلُ مِنْهُ كُلَّ يَوْمٍ خَمْسَ
مَرَّاتٍ هَلْ يَبْقَى مِنْ دَرَنِهِ شَيْءٌ ؟ قَالُوا : لَا يَبْقَى مِنْ دَرَنِهِ شَيْءٌ ،
قَالَ : فَذَلِكَ مَثَلُ الصَّلَوَاتِ الْخَمْسِ يَمْحُو اللَّهُ بِهِنَّ الْخَطَايَا

**"'Say, if there were a river at the door of one of
you in which he takes a bath five times a day,
would any soiling remain on him?' They
replied, 'No soiling would be left on him.' He
said, 'That is the five (obligatory) prayers.
Allāh obliterates all sins as a result of
performing them.'"** [10]

Zakāt is soul purification,

﴿ خُذْ مِنْ أَمْوَالِهِمْ صَدَقَةً تُطَهِّرُهُمْ وَتُزَكِّيهِم بِهَا ﴾

**"Take Sadaqah (Zakāt, charity) from their
wealth to purify them and sanctify them with
it."** [*Sūrah At-Tawbah* 9:103]

Fasting is soul purification:

﴿ يَا أَيُّهَا الَّذِينَ ءَامَنُوا كُتِبَ عَلَيْكُمُ الصِّيَامُ كَمَا كُتِبَ عَلَى
الَّذِينَ مِن قَبْلِكُمْ لَعَلَّكُمْ تَتَّقُونَ ۝ ﴾

---

[10] Reported by Muslim No. (667). It was graded Sahih.

"O you who believe! Observing As-Saum (the fasting) is prescribed for you as it was prescribed for those before you, that you may become Al-Muttaqūn (the pious)." [*Sūrah Al-Baqarah* 2:183]

Performing Hajj is also a means for soul purification.

All acts of worship prescribed by Allāh are related to this matter. Allāh (سُبْحَانَهُوَتَعَالَى) says,

"Indeed, whosoever purifies himself (by avoiding polytheism and accepting Islāmic Monotheism) shall achieve success, ○ And remembers (glorifies) the Name of his Lord (worships none but Allāh), and prays (the five compulsory prayers and the supererogatory prayers)." [*Sūrah Al-'A'lā* 87:14-15]

Remembering Allāh is remarkably the most efficient way for self-purification. The prescribed forms of remembrance have many worldly effects as well as in the Hereafter for those who observe them. They serve to purify the soul from vices. There is a hadīth in this regard related by Tirmidhī that the Prophet (صَلَّىٱللَّهُعَلَيْهِوَسَلَّمَ) passed by a tree with dry leaves, so he struck it with his staff, making the leaves fall. Then he (صَلَّىٱللَّهُعَلَيْهِوَسَلَّمَ) said,

إِنَّ الْحَمْدُ لِلَّهِ وَسُبْحَانَ اللَّهِ وَلَا إِلَهَ إِلَّا اللَّهُ وَاللَّهُ أَكْبَرُ لَتُسَاقِطُ
مِنْ ذُنُوبِ الْعَبْدِ كَمَا تَسَاقَطَ وَرَقُ هَذِهِ الشَّجَرَةِ

**"Indeed, [saying] 'Praise be to Allāh'
(alhamdulillah), 'Glory be to Allāh'
(Subhānallāh), 'There is no god worthy of
worship but Allāh.' (La ilāha ill Allah), and
'Allāh is the Greatest' (Allāhu Akbar) cause the
sins to fall from the worshipper, just as the
leaves of this tree fall."** [11]

Generally speaking, all acts of worship are means to
purify the human self.

Furthermore, abstention from prohibitions and major
sins leads to self-purification. If one did bad deeds
and vices, he would corrupt his own self. Allāh
(سُبْحَانَهُ وَتَعَالَى) says,

﴿ قُل لِّلْمُؤْمِنِينَ يَغُضُّوا مِنْ أَبْصَارِهِمْ وَيَحْفَظُوا فُرُوجَهُمْ ذَلِكَ
أَزْكَى لَهُمْ إِنَّ اللَّهَ خَبِيرٌ بِمَا يَصْنَعُونَ ۝ ﴾

**"Tell the believing men to lower their gaze
(from looking at forbidden things), and protect
their private parts (from illegal sexual acts,
etc.). That is purer for them. Verily, Allāh is**

---

[11] Reported by at-Tirmidhi No. (3533). It was graded Hasan.

All-Aware of what they do." [*Sūrah An-Nūr* 24:30]

In the same lines, Allāh says,

﴿ فَإِن لَّمْ تَجِدُوا فِيهَآ أَحَدًا فَلَا تَدْخُلُوهَا حَتَّىٰ يُؤْذَنَ لَكُمْ وَإِن قِيلَ لَكُمُ ارْجِعُوا فَارْجِعُوا هُوَ أَزْكَىٰ لَكُمْ وَاللَّهُ بِمَا تَعْمَلُونَ عَلِيمٌ ﴿٢٨﴾ ﴾

"And if you find no one therein, still, enter not until permission has been given. And if you are asked to go back, go back, for it is purer for you. And Allāh is All-Knower of what you do." [*Sūrah An-Nūr* 24:28]

Third: Self-purification by doing desirable acts. In the following *Qudsi* Hadīth, Allāh (سُبْحَانَهُ وَتَعَالَى) says,

وَمَا تَقَرَّبَ إِلَيَّ عَبْدِي بِشَيْءٍ أَحَبَّ إِلَيَّ مِمَّا افْتَرَضْتُ عَلَيْهِ ، وَمَا يَزَالُ عَبْدِي يَتَقَرَّبُ إِلَيَّ بِالنَّوَافِلِ حَتَّى أُحِبَّهُ ؛ فَإِذَا أَحْبَبْتُهُ كُنْتُ سَمْعَهُ الَّذِي يَسْمَعُ بِهِ ، وَبَصَرَهُ الَّذِي يُبْصِرُ بِهِ ، وَيَدَهُ الَّتِي يَبْطِشُ بِهَا ، وَرِجْلَهُ الَّتِي يَمْشِي بِهَا ، وَإِنْ سَأَلَنِي لَأُعْطِيَنَّهُ وَلَئِنِ اسْتَعَاذَنِي لَأُعِيذَنَّهُ

"And the most beloved thing with which My servant comes nearer to Me is what I have enjoined upon him, and My servant keeps on coming closer to Me through performing Nawafil (prayer or doing extra deeds besides what is obligatory) till I love him. When I love him, I become his hearing with which he hears, his seeing with which he sees, his hand with which he strikes, and his leg with which he walks; and if he asks (something) from Me, I give him, and if he asks My Protection (refuge), I protect him." [12]

In short, self-purification can be summed in three aspects:

First: Monotheism and faith in Allāh and His commands.

Second: Self-purification by doing righteous good deeds and abstention from prohibitions.

Third: Self-purification by doing desirable and recommended acts.

Ibn Al-Qayyim (رحمه الله) said in his "Madārij As-Sālikīn,"

---

[12] Reported by al-Bukhari No. (6502). It was graded Sahih.

"Self-purification is best conveyed by the Prophets (عَلَيْهِمُ السَّلَامُ). They were the role models in self-purification so as to teach, clarify and guide people. It was by no means natural to them. They are sent for curing souls of mankind. Allāh (سُبْحَانَهُ وَتَعَالَى) says,

﴿ هُوَ ٱلَّذِى بَعَثَ فِى ٱلْأُمِّيِّنَ رَسُولًا مِّنْهُمْ يَتْلُوا۟ عَلَيْهِمْ ءَايَـٰتِهِۦ وَيُزَكِّيهِمْ وَيُعَلِّمُهُمُ ٱلْكِتَـٰبَ وَٱلْحِكْمَةَ وَإِن كَانُوا۟ مِن قَبْلُ لَفِى ضَلَـٰلٍ مُّبِينٍ ۝ ﴾

"He it is Who sent among the unlettered ones a Messenger (Muḥammad (صَلَّى اللَّهُ عَلَيْهِ وَسَلَّمَ)) from among themselves, reciting to them His Verses, purifying them (from the filth of disbelief and polytheism), and teaching them the Book (this Qurʾān, Islāmic laws and Islāmic jurisprudence) and Al-Hikmah (As-Sunnah: legal ways, orders, acts of worship of Prophet Muḥammad (صَلَّى اللَّهُ عَلَيْهِ وَسَلَّمَ)). And verily, they had been before in manifest error." [*Sūrah Al-Jumuʿah* 62:2]

And Allāh (سُبْحَانَهُ وَتَعَالَى) says,

$$\{\,كَمَآ أَرْسَلْنَا فِيكُمْ رَسُولًا مِّنكُمْ يَتْلُوا عَلَيْكُمْ ءَايَـٰتِنَا وَيُزَكِّيكُمْ وَيُعَلِّمُكُمُ ٱلْكِتَـٰبَ وَٱلْحِكْمَةَ وَيُعَلِّمُكُم مَّا لَمْ تَكُونُوا تَعْلَمُونَ ١٥١\,\}$$

"Similarly, (to complete My Blessings on you), We have sent among you a Messenger (Muḥammad صَلَّى ٱللَّهُ عَلَيْهِ وَسَلَّمَ) of your own, reciting to you Our Verses (the Qur'ān) and purifying you, and teaching you the Book (the Qur'ān) and the Hikmah (i.e. Sunnah, Islāmic laws and Fiqh – jurisprudence), and teaching you that which you used not to know." [*Sūrah Al-Baqarah* 2:151]

Sufyan Ibn 'Uyaynah (رَحِمَهُ ٱللَّهُ) said,

"The Prophet (صَلَّى ٱللَّهُ عَلَيْهِ وَسَلَّمَ) is the criterion against which all deeds are measured. All acts must be measured against his manners and behavior. Whatever is consistent with them is approved but whatever contradicts them is disapproved."

This is extremely critical to self-purification. One should purify himself by following the Prophet (صَلَّى ٱللَّهُ عَلَيْهِ وَسَلَّمَ). All deeds must be consistent with the

Sunnah of the Prophet (ﷺ). Ibn al-Qayyim (رحمه الله) said,

> "Self-purification is harder than curing bodies. Whoever purifies himself with the kind of training and solitude unsanctioned by the Messengers of Allāh is like the patient who wants to seeks remedy without any medical consultation. Messengers are the hearts' curers. Hence, the only means to self-purification is to follow the Prophets and submit to them."

Some people think that one's soul can be purified by pressuring and depriving oneself of its natural needs that Allāh made necessary to have. The Prophet (ﷺ) said,

لِنَفْسِكَ عَلَيْكَ حَقٌّ

"Give your body its right."[13]

Some people believe soul purification is achieved by depriving oneself from its lawful needs or by forcing oneself and recklessness. Such are useless means to attain soul purification. It can be obtained through committing to the moderation of the guidance of the Prophet (ﷺ); free of extremism and negligence.

---

[13] Reported by at-Tirmidhi No. (2413). It was graded Sahih.

Moderation in this particular situation is a must. Indeed, people take different means; some people choose extreme approaches and impose unjustifiable strictness. The Prophet (ﷺ) said,

إِنَّ الدِّينَ يُسْرٌ، وَلَنْ يُشَادَّ الدِّينَ أَحَدٌ إِلَّا غَلَبَهُ، فَسَدِّدُوا وَقَارِبُوا وَأَبْشِرُوا

"Indeed, the religion of Islām is very easy, and no one will ever overburden himself in religion except that it will overcome him. So, seek what is appropriate, and come as close as you can, and receive the glad tidings (that you will be rewarded)." [14]

Other people purify themselves by ways and means unsanctioned by the Sunnah. Tracking people's approaches to achieve this objective reveals they are either extremist or negligent. However, the proper means is moderation.

Ibn Al-Qayyim (رَحِمَهُ ٱللَّهُ) noted in his book (Madārij As-Sālikīn):

"When the soul deviates, it adopts one of two bad ways without a third. Deviation from humility, for example, ends up either with arrogance or meanness. Deviation from

---

[14] Reported by an-Nasā'ī No. (5034). It was graded Sahih.

shyness ends up with either rudeness or cowardice. Furthermore, deviation from patience ends up with either excessive sorrow or mercilessness. Deviation from deliberateness ends up with either total indiscretion or overall violence. Deviation from dignity Allāh granted to people of faith ends up with either vanity or lowliness. At last, deviation from the bravery ends up with either rashness or cowardice."

Therefore, to purify the soul, one should do no more or less than to follow the steps of the Prophet (ﷺ), who adopted moderation, free from extremism and negligence.

It is advisable to know that the best righteous deeds are the ones that follow the way of Allāh and from which one can benefit. These types of righteous deeds may be the easiest and may be the most difficult. Admittedly, every difficult act is not necessarily good, nor every good deed is necessarily easy. If our religion directed us to do something seemingly difficult, it is for the sake of the embedded benefit, not to make us suffer. The Prophet (ﷺ) said,

إِنَّمَا بُعِثْتُمْ مُيَسِّرِينَ وَلَمْ تُبْعَثُوا مُعَسِّرِينَ

"You have been sent to facilitate and not create difficulties." [15]

The Prophet said to Mu'ādh and Abu Mousa (رَضِيَٱللَّهُعَنْهُمْ) when he sent them to Yemen,

يَسِّرَا وَلَا تُعَسِّرَا وَبَشِّرَا وَلَا تُنَفِّرَا

"Show leniency (to the people); do not be hard on them! Give them glad tidings (of Divine favors in this world and the Hereafter), and do not create aversion!" [16]

Also, the Prophet (صَلَّىٱللَّهُعَلَيْهِوَسَلَّمَ) said,

هَذَا الدِّينَ يُسْرٌ، وَلَنْ يُشَادَّ الدِّينَ أَحَدٌ إِلَّا غَلَبَهُ

"Indeed, this religion is easy, and no one will ever overburden himself in religion except that it will overcome him." [17]

The Prophet (صَلَّىٱللَّهُعَلَيْهِوَسَلَّمَ) said,

أَحَبُّ الدِّينِ إِلَى اللَّهِ الْحَنِيفِيَّةُ السَّمْحَةُ

---

[15] Reported by al-Bukhari No. (220). It was graded Sahih.
[16] Reported by Muslim No. (1733). It was graded Sahih.
[17] Reported by an-Nasā'ī No. (5034). It was graded Sahih.

"Allāh likes the deeds best when they are consistent with the simple, easy-going Hanifiyyah." [18]

Satan has his means to interfere in one's attempt at soul purification. When Satan notices one attempting to purify himself, he deludes him to either follow the extreme way through abandoning desirable acts and eating less food or turn one away from the true path. One should commit with the Islāmic laws and the Sunnah of the Prophet (ﷺ) and to keep away from anything prohibited.

- In this regard, one helpful means that must be highlighted is to remember always that one will stand before Allāh and will be held accountable. Allāh (سُبْحَانَهُوَتَعَالَى) says,

﴿ يَٰٓأَيُّهَا ٱلَّذِينَ ءَامَنُواْ ٱتَّقُواْ ٱللَّهَ وَلۡتَنظُرۡ نَفۡسٞ مَّا قَدَّمَتۡ لِغَدٖ ﴾

"O you who believe! Fear Allāh and keep your duty to Him. And let every person look to what he has sent forth for the morrow." [*Sūrah Al-Hashr* 59:18]

And Allāh (سُبْحَانَهُوَتَعَالَى) says,

---

[18] Al-Adab al-Mufrad Hadith No. (287). Shaykh al-Albaani graded it to be Hasan.

﴿ يَـٰٓأَيُّهَا ٱلَّذِينَ ءَامَنُوا۟ قُوٓا۟ أَنفُسَكُمْ وَأَهْلِيكُمْ نَارًا وَقُودُهَا ٱلنَّاسُ وَٱلْحِجَارَةُ عَلَيْهَا مَلَـٰٓئِكَةٌ غِلَاظٌ شِدَادٌ ﴾

"O you who believe! Ward off from yourselves and your families a Fire (Hell) whose fuel is men and stones, over which are (appointed) angels stern (and) severe." [Sūrah At-Tahrīm 66:6]

And concerning the last verses sent down upon the Prophet (صَلَّىٰ ٱللَّهُ عَلَيْهِ وَسَلَّمَ). Allāh (سُبْحَانَهُ وَتَعَالَىٰ) says,

﴿ وَٱتَّقُوا۟ يَوْمًا تُرْجَعُونَ فِيهِ إِلَى ٱللَّهِ ثُمَّ تُوَفَّىٰ كُلُّ نَفْسٍ مَّا كَسَبَتْ ﴾

"And be afraid of the Day when you shall be brought back to Allāh. Then every person shall be paid what he earned." [Sūrah Al-Baqarah 2:281]

According to a hadīth whose authenticity is questionable, however, its meaning is undoubtedly correct,

الْكَيِّسُ مَنْ دَانَ نَفْسَهُ وَعَمِلَ لِمَا بَعْدَ الْمَوْتِ ، وَالْعَاجِزُ مَنْ أَتْبَعَ نَفْسَهُ هَوَاهَا وَتَمَنَّى عَلَى اللَّهِ الأماني

"The wise man is the one who takes account of himself and strives for that which after death. And the helpless man is the one who follows his own whims then indulges in wishful thinking about Allāh." [19]

The word *wise* describes the knowledgeable man who takes account of himself and prepares himself for that which is after death. In contrast, the helpless man is the one who follows his own whims then indulges in wishful thinking about Allāh.

Finally, the one whom Allāh blessed with piety and uprightness should always keep in mind that he's only who he is due to the grace of Allāh. Without it, he will not be guided. One should not look upon himself with admiration. Allāh (سُبْحَانَهُوَتَعَالَ) says,

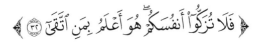

"So, ascribe not purity to yourselves. He knows best him who fears Allāh and keep his duty to Him [i.e. those who are Al-Muttaqūn (the pious)]." [*Sūrah An-Najm* 53:32]

And Allāh (سُبْحَانَهُوَتَعَالَ) says,

---

[19] Reported by Ibn Majah in his Sunan No. (4401). It was graded Da'īf.

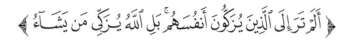

"Have you not seen those who claim sanctity for themselves? Nay, but Allāh sanctifies whom He pleases." [*Sūrah An-Nisā' 4:49*]

So, if one is guided to this guidance of Allāh and uprightness, he should be grateful to Allāh without having any feeling of self-conceit. Allāh (سُبْحَانَهُوَتَعَالَ) mentioned the traits of true believers,

﴿ وَٱلَّذِينَ يُؤْتُونَ مَآ ءَاتَوا وَّقُلُوبُهُمْ وَجِلَةٌ أَنَّهُمْ إِلَىٰ رَبِّهِمْ رَٰجِعُونَ ۝ ﴾

"And those who give that (their charity) which they give (and also do other good deeds) with their hearts full of fear (whether their alms and charities, etc., have been accepted or not), because they are sure to return to their Lord (for reckoning)." [*Sūrah Al-Mu'minūn 23:60*]

Meaning they are doing righteous good deeds, but they are afraid. On the authority of 'Aisha (رَضِيَٱللَّهُعَنْهَا) who asked the Prophet (صَلَّىٱللَّهُعَلَيْهِوَسَلَّمَ) about the meaning of the above verse,

أَهُوَ الَّذِي يَزْنِي وَيَسْرِقُ وَيَشْرَبُ الْخَمْرَ؟ قَالَ لَا يَا بِنْتَ أَبِي بَكْرٍ
أَوْ يَا بِنْتَ الصِّدِّيقِ ؛ وَلَكِنَّهُ الرَّجُلُ يَصُومُ وَيَتَصَدَّقُ وَيُصَلِّي وَهُوَ
يَخَافُ أَنْ لَا يُتَقَبَّلَ مِنْهُ

"'O Messenger of Allāh! [Does it refer to] the one who commits adultery, steals, and drinks alcohol?' He said, 'No, O daughter of Abu Bakr – O daughter of Siddiq – rather it is a man who fasts, gives charity and prays, but fears that those will not be accepted from him.'"

Thus, Al-Hassan al-Basri (رَحِمَهُٱللَّهُ) said:

"A true believer is always concerned when he does good deeds, whereas the hypocrite feels secure and does evil deeds."

The believer does righteous good deeds, but feels concerned they may not be accepted, while the hypocrite does evil deeds, yet he is assured they will be accepted.

The Muslim should strive to do righteous good deeds, seek the pleasure of Allāh, and reproach himself in case of negligence. One should make efforts to keep away from sins and prohibitions that deprive him of blessings and good in this worldly life and the life to come. One should fear Allāh's torment and hope for Allāh's Mercy:

﴿ أُوْلَٰٓئِكَ ٱلَّذِينَ يَدْعُونَ يَبْتَغُونَ إِلَىٰ رَبِّهِمُ ٱلْوَسِيلَةَ أَيُّهُمْ
أَقْرَبُ وَيَرْجُونَ رَحْمَتَهُۥ وَيَخَافُونَ عَذَابَهُۥٓ إِنَّ عَذَابَ رَبِّكَ كَانَ
مَحْذُورًا ۝ ﴾

"Those whom they call upon [like 'Isā (Jesus) -
son of Maryam (Mary), 'Uzayr (Ezra), angel,
etc.] desire (for themselves) means of access to
their Lord (Allah), as to which of them should
be the nearest and they ['Isā (Jesus), 'Uzayr
(Ezra), angels, etc.] hope for His Mercy and fear
His Torment. Verily, the Torment of your Lord
is something to be afraid of!" [*Sūrah Al-'Isrā'*
17:57]

I beseech Allāh, the Most Gracious, the Lord of the
Mighty Throne, with His Gracious Names and
Attributes, and that none has the right to be
worshipped but Allāh, Who infused His mercy and
knowledge in everything, to grant us success, to set
our matters right, and to forgive us, our fathers, our
scholars and the Muslims, men and women, dead and
alive. O Allāh! Grant me piety and purify my soul as
You are the Best to purify it. You are its Guardian and
its Protecting Friend. O Allāh! Give us help and
victory and do not give anyone victory upon us. O
Allāh! Plot on our side, not against us. O Allāh! Guide
us and grant us victory upon who attacked us. O

Allāh! Make us grateful to You and from those who remember You with humility. O Allāh! Accept our repentance and purify our souls and set firm our feet and guide our hearts and remove the hatred from our hearts. O Allāh! Unite our hearts, guide us to the ways of peace and bring us out from darkness into light; bless us in our hearing, vision, wives, sons, money, time and make us blessed wherever we are. O Allāh! Make us safe in our countries and set our kings right. O Allāh! Guide our kings to every goodness. O Ever-living, O Sustainer! Guide them to everything you like of righteous good deeds. O Allāh! Your mercy is what I hope for. Do not abandon me to myself for an instant, but put all my affairs in good order for me; there is none who has the right to be worshiped but You alone. Praise be to Allāh, first and last. May Allāh's prayers and blessings be upon His servant and Messenger Muḥammad (ﷺ) and his family and Companions.

QUESTIONS

Question: His Eminence Shaykh, I love you for the sake of Allāh. We are undergraduate students and seek your advice. There is another question with the same objective that says, "We are from France, and we seek your advice." It will be translated into French, may Allāh bless you?

Answer: First, I love you for the sake of Allāh; may Allāh make us from those who love for the sake of Allāh, and guide us all to righteous good deeds. My meeting with you is considered an advice to the brother, myself and us all. Seeking soul purification is important. The true believer should seek this purification. O, brothers! It's hard to know precisely what kind of advice the questioner wants, but there is a beneficial narration we should bear in mind and translate and publish it. A man sent a message to Abdullāh Ibn 'Umar (رَضِيَٱللَّهُعَنْهُ) saying, "Write down all the knowledge for me!" What do you think of this question? When a great scholar is asked this question, what should he say? Abdullāh Ibn 'Umar sent to him saying, "Knowledge is so wide, but if you can meet Allāh with no blood on your hands, no stealing or insulting Muslims, you should do it." If you can adhere to these three aspects, you will earn all types of goodness. These three points mentioned by

Abdullāh Ibn 'Umar (رَضِيَاللَّهُعَنْهُمَ) were also highlighted by
the Prophet (صَلَّاللَّهُعَلَيْهِوَسَلَّمَ) in his Farewell Khutbah,
which was delivered during Hajj that featured a huge
crowd. The Prophet (صَلَّاللَّهُعَلَيْهِوَسَلَّمَ) said to them:

أَيُّ يَوْمٍ هَذَا ؟ .. أَيُّ بَلَدٍ هَذَا ؟ .. أَيُّ شَهْرٍ هَذَا ؟ ثم قال عليه
الصلاة والسلام: فَإِنَّ دِمَاءَكُمْ وَأَمْوَالَكُمْ وَأَعْرَاضَكُمْ
عَلَيْكُمْ حَرَامٌ كَحُرْمَةِ يَوْمِكُمْ هَذَا فِي بَلَدِكُمْ هَذَا فِي شَهْرِكُمْ
هَذَا

"Do you know what day today is? Do you
what town is this town? Do you know what
month is this month? Then he (صَلَّاللَّهُعَلَيْهِوَسَلَّمَ) said,
"Your blood, property, and honor are
sanctified and cannot be violated by one
another (i.e. Muslims) like the sanctity of this
day of yours, in this month of yours and the
city of yours." [20]

These three matters are imperative for Muslims:
hurting no Muslim even to the extent of a small
wound or a drop of blood, meeting Allāh with no
illegally-earned money using transgression, and
meeting Allāh after ceasing to speak ill of Muslims.
This advice is very beneficial and useful.

---

[20] Reported by al-Bukhari No. (6043). It was graded Sahih.

Another question: An Imām asks, "Which book do you advise to be taught for the general public in the Masjid that tackles the actions, illnesses of the heart and their cure, in connection with the creed of Ahlus-Sunnah?"

Answer: In reality, the book of Riyādh Ṣālihīn by An-Nawawī (رحمه الله) is beneficial in this respect. It is a readable book in which Imām Nawawī compiled many aḥādīth. And many Imāms in Masjids teach the Muslims this book. But it is important to read the scholars' commentaries to clarify the meanings of the aḥādīth. It is worth noting that Shaykh Ibn Uthaymeen (رحمه الله) made an explanation of this book, upon which he made fruitful comments. The book is printed and published. Also, there are many small and big books, of which a valuable book by Ibn al-Qayyim called "A Message of Ibn al-Qayyim to One of His Brothers." It is a precious book, and it is very short to the extent you can finish reading it in half an hour.

Question: Our eminent Shaykh, in Madārij As-Sālikīn by Ibn al-Qayyim, I read on the topic of trust in Allāh that the sinner has trust in Allāh when committing sins. It is known that trust in Allāh is an act of worship; is he rewarded for this? How can we understand this text?

Answer: According to the scholars, trust in Allāh is enjoined in every state and deed, in worldly and religious matters. Thus, the Prophet (ﷺ) advised he who leaves his house, whether for religious or worldly purposes to say,

بِسْمِ اللهِ تَوَكَّلْتُ عَلَى اللهِ ، لَا حَوْلَ وَ لَا قُوَّةَ إِلَّا بِاللهِ. قَالَ: فَإِذَا يُقَالُ حِينَئِذٍ هُدِيتَ وَكُفِيتَ وَوُقِيتَ فَتَتَنَحَّى لَهُ الشَّيَاطِينُ فَيَقُولُ لَهُ شَيْطَانٌ آخَرُ كَيْفَ لَكَ بِرَجُلٍ قَدْ هُدِيَ وَكُفِيَ وَوُقِيَ

"'I begin with the Name of Allāh; I trust in Allāh; there is no altering of conditions but by the Power of Allāh.' He said, 'If he said this, it would be said to him, 'You are guided, defended and protected.' The devil will go far away from him. And say to another devil, 'How can you deal with a man who has been guided, defended, and protected?'" [21]

Muslims should keep away from sins and abstain from prohibitions. If anyone uses the lawful means to do evil deeds, he will become indulged in prohibitions, and Allāh will punish him. Thus, one should always trust in Allāh, seek refuge with Allāh, and one should trust in Allāh in doing righteous good deeds and keeping away from sins.

---

[21] Reported by Abi Dawud No. (5095). It was graded Sahih.

Question: A question about the phrase **"We seek Your guidance;"** is it authentically narrated in the Khutbah of need?

Answer: It means that one seeks guidance; this is a great supplication that the Muslim should pray for Allāh to grant. Thus, this supplication is repeated seventeen times a day to ask Allāh's guidance:

﴿ إِيَّاكَ نَعْبُدُ وَإِيَّاكَ نَسْتَعِينُ ۝ اهْدِنَا الصِّرَاطَ الْمُسْتَقِيمَ ۝ ﴾

"You (Alone) we worship, and You (Alone) we ask for help (for each and everything. Guide us to the Straight Way." [*Sūrah Al-Fātihah* 1:5-6]

This supplication **"Guide us to the Straight Way,"** is repeated seventeen times during one's prayers, which is equivalent to the number of Raka in the prayers. Also, the Khutbah of need reads as follows,

إِنَّ الْحَمْدَ للهِ نَحْمَدُهُ وَ نَسْتَعِينُهُ وَ نَسْتَغْفِرُهُ وَ نَتُوبُ إِلَيْهِ وَ نَعُوذُ بِاللهِ مِنْ شُرُورِ أَنْفُسِنَا وَ سَيِّئَاتِ أَعْمَالِنَا.

"Praise be to Allāh, we praise Him, we seek His help. We seek refuge with Allāh from the evil of our own souls and our bad deeds."

So, seeking guidance from Allāh is a great supplication.

Question: Our Shaykh I love you for the sake of Allāh. I'm a knowledge seeker, but I suffer from a sin I commit when I'm alone. Then I repent and weep, but I do it again after a while. I became unable to seek knowledge though I like seeking it, but this sin hinders me. What can I do, may Allāh bless you! I am afraid to meet Allāh committing this crime.

Answer: First of all, I ask Allāh to guide us to the Straight Way, and we seek refuge in Him from the evil of our own souls and from our bad deeds and to set our matters right. O, brother! It is advisable to remember Allāh all the time. Shaykh Shinqiti (رَحِمَهُ ٱللَّٰه) said, "All scholars agreed that the best way to abstain is to know that Allāh sees you."

It is said,

إذا خلوت الدهر يوما فلا تقل خلوتُ ولكن قل عليّ رقيب

"If you were alone one day, do not say

I am alone, but Allāh is watching over me."

At-Tirmidhi related that the Prophet (صَلَّى ٱللَّٰهُ عَلَيْهِ وَسَلَّمَ) said,

اسْتَحْيُوا مِنْ اللَّهِ حَقَّ الْحَيَاءِ

"Have shyness from Allāh in a manner that it is His due."

The most required type of shyness is that for Allāh, the Lord of the worlds. When one is alone, a Muslim should remember Allāh and know that Allāh sees him,

$$﴿ يَعۡلَمُ ٱلسِّرَّ وَأَخۡفَى ۝ ﴾$$

"He knows the secret and that which is yet more hidden." [*Sūrah Tāhā* 20:7]

And,

$$﴿ يَعۡلَمُ خَآئِنَةَ ٱلۡأَعۡيُنِ وَمَا تُخۡفِى ٱلصُّدُورُ ۝ ﴾$$

"Allāh knows the fraud of the eyes, and all that the breasts conceal." [*Sūrah Ghāfir* 40:19]

One should not act in his solitude in the same manner Allāh describes:

$$﴿ يَسۡتَخۡفُونَ مِنَ ٱلنَّاسِ وَلَا يَسۡتَخۡفُونَ مِنَ ٱللَّهِ وَهُوَ مَعَهُمۡ إِذۡ يُبَيِّتُونَ مَا لَا يَرۡضَىٰ مِنَ ٱلۡقَوۡلِ ﴾$$

"They may hide (their crimes) from men, but they cannot hide (them) from Allāh; for He is

with them (by His Knowledge) when they plot by night in words that He does not approve." [*Sūrah An-Nisā'* 4:108]

One should fear Allāh when being alone. If his soul intrigues him to commit a sin, he should remember that Allāh sees him and Allāh (سُبْحَانَهُوَتَعَالَى) is All-Knowing, All-Hearer, All-Seer, Most-Acquainted. Luqmān, the wise man, advised his son,

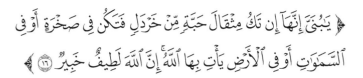

"O, my son! If it is (anything) equal to the weight of a grain of mustard-seed, and though it is in a rock, or in the heavens or the earth, Allah will bring it forth. Verily, Allah is Subtle (in bringing out that grain), Well-Aware (of its place)." [*Sūrah Luqmān* 31:16]

Be careful that you will meet Allāh and you will be held accountable, and your deeds will be shown on the Day of Resurrection.

﴿ وَوَجَدُواْ مَا عَمِلُواْ حَاضِرًا وَلَا يَظْلِمُ رَبُّكَ أَحَدًا ۝ ﴾

"And they will find all that they did place before them, and your Lord treats no one with injustice." [*Sūrah Al-Kahf* 18:49]

What benefit would one gain if he were to obey his desires and lusts, but then comes to a bad end? It is said,

"Desires fade away from who experienced it, but sins and shame are what remain

their bad consequences are what last

no good in a desire which will be followed by hellfire."

What good is it if illegal desires are followed by punishment in this life and the life to come. The Muslim should fear Allāh and reprimand himself with Qur'ān and the admonitions it contains. The best advice is to know that Allāh sees you. Allāh (سُبْحَانَهُوَتَعَالَى) says,

$$﴿ يَٰٓأَيُّهَا ٱلَّذِينَ ءَامَنُواْ ٱتَّقُواْ ٱللَّهَ وَلْتَنظُرْ نَفْسٌ مَّا قَدَّمَتْ لِغَدٍ وَٱتَّقُواْ ٱللَّهَ إِنَّ ٱللَّهَ خَبِيرٌ بِمَا تَعْمَلُونَ ۝ ﴾$$

"O, you who believe! Fear Allāh and keep your duty to Him. And let every person look to what has sent forth for the morrow, and fear Allāh.

Verily, Allāh is All-Aware of what you do."
[*Sūrah Al-Hashr* 59:18]

Question: Is it sufficient to seek Allāh's forgiveness from acts of polytheism in a general manner or is it necessary to seek Allāh's forgiveness for every single act, may Allāh bless you?

Answer: It is not conditional to seek Allāh's forgiveness from every individual sin because it is highly unlikely to remember all sins. No one can remember all that he did last week? He may forget them. Allāh (سُبْحَانَهُوَتَعَالَى) says,

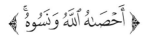

"Allāh has kept account of it, while they have forgotten it." [*Sūrah Al-Mujādilah* 58:6]

It is important to seek sincere forgiveness from all sins either known or unknown, forgotten or not, from all sins and illegal acts; whether it is *polytheism* or other sins. If one seeks forgiveness from all sins, Allāh will forgive him, because repentance removes all the past sins if one were to be sincere in his request for forgiveness. Allāh (سُبْحَانَهُوَتَعَالَى) says,

﴿ ۞ قُل يَٰعِبَادِىَ ٱلَّذِينَ أَسْرَفُوا۟ عَلَىٰٓ أَنفُسِهِمْ لَا تَقْنَطُوا۟ مِن رَّحْمَةِ ٱللَّهِ إِنَّ ٱللَّهَ يَغْفِرُ ٱلذُّنُوبَ جَمِيعًا ﴾

"Say: "O 'Ibadi (My slaves) who have transgressed against themselves (by committing evil deeds and sins)! Despair not of the Mercy of Allah, verily Allah forgives all sins. Truly, He is Oft-Forgiving, Most Merciful." [*Sūrah Az-Zumar* 39:53]

Meaning polytheism, sins, and every falsehood. Whoever seeks sincere forgiveness, Allāh will forgive him. There are forms of forgiveness that tackle this matter in detail such as in the Prophet's (صَلَّىٱللَّهُعَلَيْهِوَسَلَّمَ) saying,

اللَّهُمَّ اغْفِرْ لِي ذَنْبِي كُلَّهُ دِقَّهُ وَجِلَّهُ وَأَوَّلَهُ وَآخِرَهُ وَعَلَانِيَتَهُ وَسِرَّهُ

"O Allāh! Forgive all my sins, the small and the great, the first and the last, the open and the secret."[22]

And he (صَلَّىٱللَّهُعَلَيْهِوَسَلَّمَ) said,

اللَّهُمَّ اغْفِرْ لِي مَا قَدَّمْتُ وَمَا أَخَّرْتُ وَمَا أَسْرَرْتُ وَمَا أَعْلَنْتُ وَمَا أَسْرَفْتُ وَمَا أَنْتَ أَعْلَمُ بِهِ مِنِّي

---

[22] Reported by Muslim No. (483). It was graded Sahih.

"O Allāh! Grant me forgiveness from the faults, which I did in haste or deferred, which I committed in privacy or public and You are better aware (of them) than myself."

Also, narrated Shaddād (رَضِيَاللَّهُعَنْهُ),

وَأَسْتَغْفِرُكَ لِمَا تَعْلَمُ إِنَّكَ أَنْتَ عَلَّامُ الْغُيُوبِ

"And I seek your forgiveness for what You know. Verily, You are the Knower of all that what is hidden." [23]

If this kind of forgiveness is sincere and made for all one's sins, even without the need to mention individual crimes, Allāh will forgive all sins because Allāh is Oft-Forgiving, Most Merciful.

Question: What is the rule that distinguishes narratives about Allāh from Allāh's Attributes; may Allāh bless you?

Answer: Narratives about Allāh are more comprehensive than Attributes and Attributes are more comprehensive than Allāh's Names. This rule is related to the knowledge of Allāh's Names and Attributes. Allāh's Names and Attributes are strictly

---

[23] Reported by at-Tirmidhi No. (3407). It was graded Sahih.

limited to those mentioned in the Qur'ān and Sunnah. We Must affirm that Allāh is All-Hearer, All-Seer.

Allāh says,

"He is the All-Hearer, the All-Seer." [*Sūrah ash-Shūrā* 42:11]

So, if any Name is found in the Qur'ān or the Sunnah, we must affirm them due to their existence in the Qur'ān and Sunnah. Allāh's Attributes are more recognizable in determining the Attributes of Allāh. One way to recognize them is through definite, straightforward descriptions of Allāh. He (سُبْحَانَهُوَتَعَالَ) says,

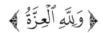

"But honor, power and glory belong to Allāh." [*Sūrah Al-Munāfiqūn* 63:8]

It is also can be recognized through the verb indicating the Attribute:

"Verily, I am with you both, hearing and seeing." [*Sūrah Tāhā* 20:46]

And,

$$ ﴿ قَدْ سَمِعَ ٱللَّهُ قَوْلَ ٱلَّتِي تُجَٰدِلُكَ فِى زَوْجِهَا وَتَشْتَكِىٓ إِلَى ٱللَّهِ وَٱللَّهُ يَسْمَعُ تَحَاوُرَكُمَآ ﴾ $$

"Indeed, Allāh has heard the statement of her (Khawlah Bint Tha'labah) that disputes with you (O Muḥammad (ﷺ)) concerning her husband (Aws bin As-Samit) and complains to Allāh. And Allāh hears the argument between you both. Verily, Allāh is All-Hearer, All-Seer." [*Sūrah Al-Mujādilah* 58:1]

In this verse, the verb indicates the Hearing of Allāh using the verb. Also, every Name of Allāh indicates an Attribute of His that is perfect from all aspects. From the name of the All-Hearer, we deduce the Attribute of Hearing; the All-Knower, the Attribute of Knowing; Most Merciful, the Attribute of Mercy; Glorious, the Attribute of Glory and so on. Allāh's Attributes are more comprehensive than Names, and narratives about Allāh are more detailed than just Attributes.

Question: Do you remember any situation of your father Shaykh Abdul Muḥsin (حفظه الله) and Shaykh Abdullah Al-Ghudayyan (رَحِمَهُ ٱللَّهُ)?

Answer: There are numerous memorable instances of the great scholars, my father or Shaykh Ghudayyan (رَحِمَهُ ٱللَّهُ) who died yesterday and his funeral prayer will be performed upon him today. I beseech Allāh to forgive him and all the Muslim scholars and the Muslims and believers, dead or alive. The life of the scholars are full of lessons and admonitions which are fruitful for the successful men, and they have beneficial knowledge based upon the Qur'ān and the Sunnah. However, I'd like to speak about my father, Shaykh Abdul Muhsin (حفظه الله). In the past few days, he finished explaining Sunan Ibn Majah in the daily lesson in the Prophetic Masjid. He started explaining the Six Books of the Sunnah in early Muharram 1406 in every day except Thursday, after Al-Maghrib. He stopped teaching during holidays. It took him twenty-six years to finish teaching and explaining the Six Books in the Prophetic Masjid. May Allāh accept his righteous good deeds and guide us to the beneficial knowledge and the righteous good deeds and guide us to the Straight Way.

I'd like to thank you for attending and your patience. I beseech Allāh to accept your good deeds. I beg Allāh to make our session beneficial and truthful and to make our deeds weigh heavy. I ask Allāh to forgive us, our fathers, our Shaykhs, the Muslims and the believers dead or alive. O Allāh! Accept our deeds, for You are All-Hearer, All-Knower. Forgive us, for You are Oft-Forgiving, Most Merciful.

May Allāh's Prayers and Blessings upon His Messenger and Servant Muḥammad (صَلَّى ٱللَّهُ عَلَيْهِ وَسَلَّمَ), his family, and Companions.

Made in the USA
Columbia, SC
26 February 2023

12985635R00048